HEAT

Series 3 Number 10

Matlok Griffiths
Mumbles & Clunks (Plate 44) 2018
monotype
31 × 23 cm (image and plate)
courtesy of the artist and
ReadingRoom, Naarm/Melbourne

Matlok Griffiths's suite of forty-four
monotypes, *Mumbles & Clunks*,
was made over six weeks when
Griffiths had access to another
artist's printing press. His journal
drawings, as well as lists of words
lifted from newspaper crosswords,
became the starting point for several
compositions in which personal
inspirations are refigured, abstracted
and transformed through techniques
of repetition and variation. The
resulting images, at once spare and
bold, bear material traces of the
artist's ever-evolving process.
Mumbles & Clunks was acquired by
the NGV in 2020 and is on display
as part of the *Melbourne Now*
exhibition at The Ian Potter Centre:
NGV Australia, Melbourne.

ISABELLA TRIMBOLI
LIFE'S WORK

She does nothing but sometimes she remembers her journal.

Alix Cléo Roubaud, *Alix's Journal*

Isabella Trimboli is a critic, essayist
and editor. Her writing on film,
literature and art has appeared in
publications such as *Metrograph
Journal*, *Sydney Review of Books*,
The Saturday Paper, *The Monthly*,
Art Guide and *The Guardian*.
She lives in Melbourne.

THE IMAGE HAS VAGUE PROVENANCE, circulating on corners of the internet that sever history and source. All we have is a caption, parroted across platforms: 'Anaïs Nin with her diaries in a bank vault, c. 1950.' If the time-stamp is correct, this was around when Anaïs was writing erotica for a dollar per page, and self-publishing experimental novels that were met with disdain, if receiving any response at all. She was spending more time in California, at the behest of Henry Miller, and would appear in Kenneth Anger's bacchanalia *The Inauguration of the Pleasure Dome* with a sparkling birdcage over her head. Her diaries were still being rejected by publishers, and it would be a decade or so before their publication would prompt the recognition she so desired.

In the black-and-white photograph, Anaïs's head and chest peek out from behind a mountain of notebooks – decades of writing from a spectacular narcissist or proto-feminist, depending on who you ask. She leans her elbows on top of the pile and her hands are pressed against her cheeks. She offers the camera a tight smile – gleeful and proud. The picture has the aura of a hunter posing with a dead animal – *look at what I've caught before it ran away!* – but in this instance, what has been snared is the shape of a life, and bits of everyday experience: dreams, affairs, agonies, friendships, and a deluge of banalities.

Earlier this year, I find the photograph. I am giving in to mindlessness, scrolling, using my hands for something other than what they are supposed to be doing – typing. But the image pierces my inattention. I save it onto my phone and send it to friends. I like the fantasy it contains: that the story of a woman's life – the one she tells, writes down, invents even – is worthy of extravagant and high-security protection. A bunch of battered notebooks treated with the same care and reverence as gleaming jewels, or government secrets.

Last year, in August, I move houses. Rent has become a burden, and I can no longer justify the big room with the balcony and the sun and the room for a desk. As I pack up my possessions, I find my life's worth of diaries, stuffed in a musty cardboard box that I have carted around with me since late adolescence.

I have been a sloppy and intermittent diarist for most of my life. But reading my journals, I found a constant spread across all of them. What I had documented was not the shape of a life, but of a self defined by the men I had been attached to. I envisioned myself purely through these romances or relationships. For long periods, this was the sole subject of my diary-keeping. In moments of being alone, or without directed desire, the diary ended without ceremony. This wasn't startling – I will always indulge in the delights of devotion or longing! – but I was upset by the diary's many absences. There were so many sadnesses and fears and joys and strange pleasures I had not thought to write down. There was only the faint sketch of great friendships or the art I was dedicated to. My imagination and my own writing had been relegated to the void. I had been a bad witness. Gloomier still, was how I'd bordered up one of the only places of personal jurisdiction, where personhood can remain perpetually open and undone.

In December and January, the work mostly dries up, as it always does. I am bored in the best way, leaning into lassitude and the shapelessness of weeks. It is boiling and sticky. I turn twenty-eight and feel weighed down by problems of living. They are basic and embarrassing problems, but impossible all the same. They are the kind that are always there, but feel more urgent and unbearable as I get older: What to do with all the desires, frivolities, and obligations that seem eternally in combat? What to do when the money keeps running out? What to do with all the clichés of male cowardice, that prove themselves clichéd for a reason, that begin to pile up around a life like an unwanted edifice, that suffocate the heart?

I decide to read the diaries of other women, other writers, to see how they worked through these eternal problems. I read them one after the other – in bed, at public pools, sprawled out on the couch, in front of the air conditioner.

Reading these journals in quick succession, their unmediated voices took up a strange form in my consciousness, a chatty and profound polyphony. It began with Helen Garner and her trilogy of diaries, astonishing in their precision, terrifying in their repetitious marital woe ('We're engaging in a bitter struggle to define ourselves, each against the other. He sets his face against things that have meaning to me, and my urge is to split hairs and demand exactitude. I suppose I'm just as unbearable to him as he is to me.'). I read Marina Tsvetaeva's poems, then seek out her Moscow diaries, where rapturous wisdom bursts from the hunger and deprivations of the Russian Revolution ('"Know thyself!" I did this. And it makes it no easier to know others. On the contrary, as soon as I begin judging another person by myself, there's just one misunderstanding after another.'). A housemate lends me Sei Shōnagon's *The Pillow Book*, where the eleventh-century lady-in-waiting exhorts her organising logic of the world through list after list – of what is difficult to speak, what is frustrating to witness, what is awkward or pointless, what is elegant and refined ('The eggs of a spot-billed duck. Shaved ice with sweet syrup, served in a shiny new metal bowl. A crystal rosary.'). A friend and I write together in the library, and one day she takes Susan Sontag's *As Consciousness Is Harnessed to Flesh* off the shelf, and whispers to me its scraps of genius. She copies down the line: 'Decline of the letter, the rise of the notebook! One doesn't write to others anymore, one writes to oneself.'

In February, I read Alix Cléo Roubaud's *Alix's Journal*. I read it because again I am scrolling, and someone posts a picture of the book, with a caption, an excerpt from the diary: 'She was exasperated, by the end of the day to have consented to the rules of others.' I am compelled by the photograph on the cover: a self-portrait of Alix, where she's twirling with a scarf around her chest. The image is faded and out of focus – mirroring how eyesight buffers under rapid movement, and the sickly discombobulation of spinning around in a circle for too long. I track down the only copy in Melbourne I can find, at a university library. I renew it again and again for the next few months.

In 1983, Alix dies from a pulmonary embolism, days after her thirty-first birthday. A year later, her husband, the Oulipo poet Jacques Roubaud, insists that Éditions du Seuil publish part of her diary; the last four years of her life in which they were together. He adds in her photographs and subtracts a few private passages. In France, it appears in 1984. In 2010, it is republished and translated into English. 'She wrote everyday, without going back, without correcting, without deleting; for herself; and perhaps, though she said nothing to this effect, neither for nor against, to be read after her death,' writes

Jacques in the book's introduction. When she moved from Canada to France in her early twenties, her diaries – which she had tended to since she was eighteen – were one of the only things she brought with her.

Alix's father was a diplomat, and she endured a peripatetic childhood that cast a long shadow of un-belonging. A severe asthmatic, she decided to study philosophy in southern France, where the weather was warm and the fresh air would benefit her delicate lungs. She started writing a dissertation on Wittgenstein but never finished. But she never relinquished his ideas about the unbridgeable gulf between what can be expressed through language and what can be expressed only through non-verbal means. In 1978, she picked up photography while trying to better her breathing at a convalescent spa in Vichy.

In *Alix's Journal*, a woman beholden to a sick body wants to loosen the bounds of corporeality, writing, art, and time. A fantasy of omniscience – 'one wished to be the only one in the world to see everything' – soaks its pages. She writes in the fragmentary form, taking up the mantle of Wittgenstein and Walter Benjamin, who she so adored. These are fragments of momentary bliss, personal theory ('There are days when one is sure that if one is better dressed, or more beautiful, in a kind of ceremonial dress if you will, one could get down to work.') and assertions on photography ('Photography is indeed a form of silence. But still a diary can show its silences, as an incomplete image its completeness.'). Then there are chronicles of the sudden suicide attempts that surprise even her, and the long stretches of despondency and chronic asthma, where she mopes around the house, unable to do anything except tear through detective novels and drink.

Her language doubles and smears, just like the bodies in her photographs. Words stutter, while punctuation warps, sometimes snapping off completely. This is heartbreaking and fidgety prose, caught between French and English, first and second person. Text and image infiltrate one another – the modalities stretch and swap. 'She took photos everyday like one imagines Victorian women kept their journal,' she writes about herself. Words spread out or compress on the page, a physical formation. Meanwhile, some of her photographs seek out the immaterial and invisible. *15 minutes at night to the rhythm of respiration* is a haze of indistinct trees that Alix captures by placing her camera on her chest, leaving the shutter open for fifteen minutes. The French writer Héléne Giannecchini, who has done the most to bring Alix out of the shadows in recent years, calls it a 'self-portrait by the breath'.

I'm interested in how Alix blends and conjoins, but never effaces herself, like I had effaced myself. All this fading and confusion, all this banishing of boundaries, and yet Alix appears, fleshy and radiant on the page. Maybe it's her ambitions that never quieten, that she acknowledges with both disgust and wonder. As well as a photographer she wants to be a writer, for her journal 'to be a draft'. But then she remembers her marriage: 'Impossibility of writing, married a poet,' she writes. Her diary is the only sovereign and free territory. She even wryly frets about her material being spread outward, untethered from her forever: 'Lively desire, upon re-reading the notebooks, to end analysis. I'm giving the best of myself there.' Beyond her husband, there doesn't seem much of an encouraging or generative milieu. Who is she surrounded by? Mostly men, often former lovers turned friends. She worked alone, exile being her established way of life.

One of these friends is the French filmmaker Jean Eustache who enacts the first public trace of her photography in his brilliant television short *Les Photos d'Alix* (1980). In the film, Alix is seated next to Jean's teenage son Boris, who asks her questions about the photos. They are straightforward and simple, of the how, when, and why variety. She responds in declarative statements that knot complexities into his line of inquiry. Her brown bob swishes gently from side to side, and a long necklace looped around her neck brushes against the table. Her speech is detached and cool, but never disinterested. I watch the film, so taken in by her casual conviction. My mind is immediately massaged into agreement; *of course*, the only real photos are childhood photos, *yes*, every photo is sentimental, and *sure*, still-life images are always of objects bound to perish. And what is a self-portrait? Everything, really.

Midway into the film, Jean, who loves to pull a prank, desynchronises image and sound. What Alix describes stops corresponding with the images laid out in front of us. We hear about a sunset, but all we see is a dark hotel room full of grimy mirrors. 'Do you recognise me?' Alix says to Boris, while pointing to a grassy field filled with plastic chairs.

Alix did not live to see the next real public trace of her work – an exhibition of *If Some Thing Black,* a series of photographs, which were shown in the summer of 1983 at Les Rencontres d'Arles. These are my favourite photographs of hers, and they appear in the last few pages of *Alix's Journal.* They are nude self-portraits, taken in an empty, barely lit room. In a few of the images, Alix is upright, light radiating off her chest. In others, she is lying corpselike on the floor. In some, her body is multiplied but fading – about to vaporise into the atmosphere.

In one photograph, she has grafted in a childhood portrait of herself, looming over her horizontal body.

Looking at these photographs, I see pre-emptive mourning, or some kind of purgatory. Lifetime is divorced from temporality or trajectory – childhood, the adult body, and the afterlife merge into one. There is a parallel found in her journal, when she writes: 'don't believe in history;to confine oneself with chronology'.

How to depict a life without the strict container of chronological time? In her diaries, Alix inspires a new notion of self-inscription, based on a restless mode of gathering and accumulation: of selves, books, beds, photographs, phone calls, tears, dresses, clouds, afternoon light, and alcoholic drinks. This is a vast, uncontrollable assemblage that cannot be defined by days alone.

Reading Alix, I think about my own journals, and how I'd forgotten all the form's freedoms and possibilities: The chance to take time in your hands. To repudiate resolution and history – and dissolve the fantasies we tell ourselves about life's sequentiality. To indulge in ongoingness, the foggy middle of experience. To coagulate one's inner world with the outer. To bend and loop language so that it gets close to the true texture of emotion, aliveness, and having a body. I'm reminded of this line by Hélène Cixous, in her famous call for *écriture féminine*: 'Time and again I, too, have felt so full of luminous torrents that I could burst with forms much more beautiful than those which are put in frames and sold for a stinking fortune.' That's what I want – a way of grappling with my life that does away with the frame, that ushers in luminous torrents.

In April, the chill has set in, but my friends and I refuse to go inside; we tremble together in flimsy coats, babbling on about flus and foolish spending and lingering disappointments and heartache. I read *Marie Bashkirtseff: The Journal of a Young Artist*. I read it because I am reading academic papers about the diary, and what they might mean for women (Cynthia Huff: diaries stress 'the bonds of our lives that are seemingly mysterious because we have been so accustomed to separating, to privileging one part of ourselves in our race to establish hierarchies.'). They are mostly dull – smothering fun, ecstatic writing under deadening analysis. But Marie, the power-hungry painter, is a constant presence on these pages. I go to the library to read the old editions of Marie's diary in their collection. It is so giant it exists in two huge volumes. They are like bibles, yellowed and mottled with brown stains.

I also look up her paintings online. They are mainly portraits, of girls who rarely glance up. Their eyes are fixed on a book in front of them, or they are assiduously sketching a nude figure in art class. She also set her gaze on the grubbier streets of Paris, painting hungry children and disobedient waifs. But despite her subjects' fates diverging cleanly down class lines, they share a look of resignation and silent anguish. Her figures are bored or sullen or exasperated, rendered in tones that reflect their youthful weariness: velvety greys, foggy greens, and patches of pale pink.

Her work – respectable, refined, if a little bland – was par for the course during Paris at the time, and Marie was duly rewarded for it. During her study at Académie Julian, one of the few private art colleges to accept female students (where Marie held a reputation for constantly munching on bonbons and bringing her pet puppy to class), she has two works accepted at the salon. In 1885, a catalogue attributed 229 works to her, but most went missing or were destroyed during World War II. Around sixty works remain. In janky digital repositories, I find the same few paintings – the gloomy women, the sodden girl clutching an umbrella and the cluster of street kids huddled around a boy with a bird's nest. In total, I count about twenty-seven works.

But in the Bibliothèque nationale de France, her nineteen-thousand-page diary, scrawled across 106 notebooks, tracing her life from thirteen years old up until her premature death at twenty-five, has been lovingly preserved. An abridged version of the journal was first published in France in 1887, at the behest of her bereaved mother, who was intimate with the solemnity and devotion of her daughter's diary keeping. One of Marie's first editors, the French author Renée d'Ulmès, wrote that this mass of notebooks was precious 'not because it describes such an entertainment or such an event, but because it reveals the mentality of a young girl'.

Marie Bashkirtseff: The Journal of a Young Artist is the diary of a relatively unknown woman, on the threshold of intellectual life and artistic glory, where dedication to truthfulness superseded shame. It was an unprecedented hit – George Bernard Shaw called it the literary sensation of its time. Then, the published diary as a genre was in its infancy, and the woman's diary was even more of an anomaly. Marie's journal was only the second diary ever to be published by a woman in France, preceded only by the bleak Catholic letter-journals of Eugénie de Guérin – the dutiful, spinster sister of radical poet Maurice de Guérin, whose writings were largely addressed to her brother and his waning spirituality.

Marie's journal broke the code. Her reputation as a painter was minor, relatively insignificant. She was not mystical or devout, doling out lessons in asceticism like Eugénie or other diarists of the time. She was not linked to any well-known writers, artists, or socialities, though she did attempt to write herself into the lives of literary figures. She sent a letter to the novelist Edmond de Goncourt, decrying his flimsy depiction of a girl's coming of age in *Chérie* (he never replied). She did manage to strike up a cunning correspondence with Guy de Maupassant, who initially thought she was a man, and then later tried to arrange some sort of tryst (she stopped replying).

Never mind, they all make their way into the journal. She mentions the two writers as people who could vouch for the diary's value and validity. This was argued in her unfinished preface to the journal, written a few months before her death, as tuberculosis tore apart her lungs. It fills in the biographical details lacking in the text. She writes of her noble, provincial origins near Poltava (present-day Ukraine) and incinerates her family members. There is her mother, who is 'ravishing' but 'ignorant of the world'. Her father, whose extramarital affairs break up her parent's marriage. Her brandy-loving Uncle, whose amoral, dodgy dealings 'destroyed us all'. There are the governesses, that teach her French and music (though she was largely self-taught, giving herself lessons on Latin, Geography and English). Then there is the trial in Russia, where her mother and aunt are implicated in, but then cleared of, colluding in the death of a brother-in-law. She writes of itinerant upbringing across Europe, where her family's wayward reputation trails her, and she becomes 'tortured by vanity'. She also stresses that if she dies young, her journal should be published.

Three years later, when the journal is published, it is received as some sort of stumbled-upon artifact of the young feminine psyche – untainted and unmediated. This is not untrue, but it fails to understand the journal's considered orchestration. Marie staked out the parameters of her writing early on in her adolescence. She would not be vain enough to self-censor. She would not let shame get in the way of vile truth. She would not think before she came to the page – as she writes in one entry, in 1876:

I never know what I'm going to write, but so much the better; there is nothing uglier than a studied journal, dressed to the hilt, especially when one is not a great writer. But I prefer my letters to those of Madame de Sévigné. 'O she ass' you exclaim. Sévigné's style is so affected, so worked over, without apparent simplicity, that it makes me sick; whereas I have no style. I make mistakes, but at least I don't adorn what I write. It is with deep conviction that I shall never be read, and with the still deeper hope of the contrary, that I write my journal.

But this propensity for no style mutates into style. The writing is breathless, sentences flung around that land in unexpected, grimy places. It is a style befitting to her subjects: her weakness for extravagant dresses, her inflamed ego, her wildly swinging moods, her despair, and her family's stained reputation. The tone of the diary is manic (but then so is adolescence, and becoming a young woman), splintering across wants and fleeting sources of attention. The French writer Maurice Barrès said that she had 'five or six exceptional souls in her delicate, already failing body'. But despite her self-obsession, she is rarely interested in asserting her individuality on the page. She is special insofar as lives, recorded, reflected upon, and self-interrogated, are always special. Another entry:

This journal is the most useful and most instructive of all writings. It's an entire life, in its smallest details, a woman with all her thoughts, hopes, deceptions, meanness, beauties, miseries, disappointments and joys. I'm not a woman yet, but I will be. It will be possible to follow me from childhood to death. The life of a person, an entire life, without any disguise or lying, is always great and interesting.

The original published journal, edited by the French poet André Theuriet and overseen by Marie's mother, cut out all damning mentions of the family's various scandals, softened her callousness towards suitors, and removed the many florid descriptions of Marie's skin and breasts, which she proclaimed, repeatedly, to be perfect. A narrative was grafted over the more protean text: of a young woman out of step with her historical moment, whose tenacity allows her to excel anyway, only for death to intervene too early. In English, restoration of the original diary only comes in the late nineties, when the academic Katherine Kernberger picks up the mantle of her late mother, who was obsessed with translating the original French text.

This arc – of a woman out of time, thwarted by illness – is too clean anyway. Marie's nature, and her insatiable, totalising ambitions, would not be well received anywhere, at any time. The diary, by its nature, is a document of time passing, but I'm interested in how Marie's journal counters the threat posed by temporality. Here is writing that chronicles a woman's mind in the present, attendant to the day-to-day. Yet this ritual is kept largely in order to outrun one's impending vanishing. The journal has one foot out the door, planted in the expanse of the future – rightfully imagining the crumbling tomb, the paintings stored away, soaked in dust. Remembrance, or legacy, then, cannot be left up to fate. It must be reverse-engineered.

Marie dies in 1884, at twenty-five, from the consumption that has trailed her for years. Fifteen years later, Mary MacLane, an American teenager living in the mining backwater of Butte, Montana, publishes a memoir, essentially her own diary. It receives similar outrage and adoration, and instantly becomes a bestseller, with hundreds of thousands of copies sold across the country. In it, she writes about loving the devil, lusting over women, and her rare, singular genius, which she proclaims has no real contemporaries. The only person she compares herself to is Marie. Later, in their adolescence, Anaïs Nin and Katherine Mansfield stumble across Marie's diary and begin to reconsider the value of their own.

In a way, I feel like Marie, tending to an impossible project, trying to cobble together 'entire' lives, in their 'smallest details' and shove them into the light. I wanted to write about these women as meticulously as they had written about themselves, return the favour in the only way I can. But I don't have a lifetime.

Impossible too is writing about the diary form. I'm chasing after something faster than me, that refuses to be pinned down. I find myself getting lost in its contradictions and capaciousness. How to write about something that is made for no one, but imagines, or hopes for, an audience anyway? Something that is off the cuff but also constructed. Unmediated but moderated by editors, publishers, partners. A way of recording and laying down a personal reality, that does not nullify multiplicity.

The self is not fixed, but reflects and refracts, appearing in innumerable variations.

In May, I watch a five-hour cut of Anne Charlotte Robertson's promethean Super 8 project *Five Year Diary*. I watch it because a friend tells me about her. She knows I am looking for diaries from women who were not writers by vocation, that had never known true recognition, that wrote about themselves obsessively and with self-scrutiny. She tells me about watching her shorts at a film festival, laughing at their mania and wit. I take the work my friends press into my hands seriously – it always has the thrill of a secret, and feels like a special embrace. I hound other friends to help me find copies of her film work.

In *Five Year Diary,* nothing really happens beyond the walls of Anne's home and garden, but that is everything and enough. What did she shoot? The moon, methodically. The making of her vegetarian meals. Her host of ever-changing, antipsychotic medications. Her family, birds, men and stone cherubs. Waterfalls and her long, mournful face, that looks as if it came straight out of an Edvard Munch painting. Like Alix – writing and photographing at the same time that Anne is filming herself – her body was her most crucial instrument, but also the source of all her self-loathing.

Longing is the diary's only organising logic. She fixates on her weight, and wishes for the arrival of her 'one true love'. She even calls her project a 'trousseau' for her future husband, an answer to what she had been doing with her life up until they fatefully meet.

When Anne began *Five Year Diary,* she was thirty-two years old, depressed and dieting, living alone in Boston,

Massachusetts. By the time of its unceremonious ending, she is forty-eight, and the diary is nearly forty hours long. She tells reporters that she had to keep going, because her movie, the movie of her life, didn't have a happy ending. But she does something more valuable here – she gives form to a life deemed formless. Anne was unmarried and childless. She was unemployed and poor. For long periods, she was a ward of the state – on disability benefits, and in and out of psych wards. Without the typical markers of a woman's or artist's life, she created new contours. She gave credence to the seemingly incidental and subordinate.

The film's run time might suggest something painfully glacial, but Anne's diary is gloriously circuitous and maniacally rhythmic. Mundane actions, sped up by time lapse, chopped and squished, have the texture of dance. Anne is a bolt of orange, speeding through her apartment, fussing about. Housework becomes an ecstatic parade of repeated, never-ending action.

I watch the diary in my bedroom, seemingly the only appropriate place to watch these intimate gestures. Anne's face fills my laptop screen, becoming part of my own life's detritus: cardigans strewn across the floor, empty mugs filled with stiff tea bags, tubes of lipstick and the silvery plastic film of medications. In the three instances where *Five Year Diary* was screened in its entirety, Anne brought her living room to the gallery, cluttering the space with notebooks, diaries and audio recordings. She described her vision as a 'home movie basement view room, a diary den, a bomb shelter, a comfortable living room filled with the artifacts from the life of a twentieth-century woman'.

In 1983, two years after Anne began *Five Year Diary*, she moves to Framingham, Massachusetts, to live with her mother.

The grim chill and slag heaps of Boston are replaced by a quieter misery, but a bigger garden. She becomes obsessed with the gazebo in the backyard, where she hoped to have her wedding someday. She would film it almost daily, tracking as the light moved with the seasons. 'Monet did his haystacks,' Anne would say later, 'and I have done the gazebo in the backyard.'

In the cut I watch, the diary lurches from this period to 1994. Anne is now forty-five years old. She is still living with her mother, still on disability benefits, and still suffering from psychosis. She plants seedlings and hides vodka in cups of orange juice. But her diary, occasionally – finally! – is being screened. 'I was so overwhelmed with what I saw,' writes Jonas Mekas, in a letter to her that year, 'I don't think it's me who is a film diarist: it's you! It's you!' But longing still orders her life. I burst into pained laughter when I watch a reel of her at the airport, where she announces to the camera: 'My film is playing at the Museum of Modern Art, and I am one hundred and ninety-five pounds!' Years later, the same old self-torture. Yet another want has been added to her list: children. Her reels are full of the engorged bellies of friends and the fascinations of children at play. She has become a doting aunt.

But then her three-year-old niece dies one morning, and the doctors have no explanation for her death. Anne has a nervous breakdown and is sent to a psych ward. Reality plummets into darkness. Anne films herself from what looks like the garden of the hospital, tear-stained and facing the camera: 'I have a right to go insane,' she says, 'I have a right to grieve.' These are despairing, difficult scenes, but they are a reminder of the many ways to mourn, the many ways to remember. When she is discharged, Anne's camera pans over her mother's overgrown garden, calling out to the dead through blooming flowers.

Anne would continue to edit and revise the diary until 1997. Then she stopped. She died fifteen years later, from lung cancer. After her death, the many reels that made up *Five Year Diary* were found pushed into the back of her bedroom closet. This was the sole copy – she had never been able to afford to print duplicates, so this single version continued to circulate sporadically, eroding each time it played.

In an article entitled 'I always liked my diary better than anything else I wrote', Helen Garner writes about her daily compulsion to record, witness and collate details; how this drive gave her the ability to write her first novel *Monkey Grip*, and how critics at the time smugly accused her of simply publishing her journal. She is hurt, but they are not wrong. I read the article years ago, but I remember it in June. I find the piece and read aloud the last paragraph to my housemates, in our icy kitchen:

What I've learnt, from editing the diaries into books and putting them out there, is that during those thousands of private hours, I'm never alone. If I go far enough, if I keep going past the boring, obedient part of me with its foot always riding the brake, and through the narrow, murky parts that are abject or angry or frightened, I find myself moving out into another region, a bigger, broader place where everybody else lives: a fearless, open-hearted firmament where images swarm, and there's music, and poetry that we almost understand, fleeting moments of sky and dirt, subtle changes in the light, a feather of a hesitation, mistakes and pain and getting over pain, all kinds of shouting and dawn and small nice things to eat, and being allowed to carry a stranger's baby round a garden, and singing in the car all the way home.

I love what this passage makes clear, what I have found so true reading all these journals: that the diary cannot be reduced to myopia or indulgence, that it is a gesture towards others, that 'open-hearted firmament' unshackled from the reins of time, or place, or bodies or death. It may be a solitary act and a private correspondence, but it is also a summoning of sorts, that can reach across an alienated expanse.

There is a line from *Alix's Journal* that seems like an explanation of what I'm trying to express on the page, right here: 'The story of what I consume is also my story.' In February, as I'm reading in bed, dazed and languid, I jot down the sentence in my phone. Months later, the line continues to haunt. I keep on repeating it to myself. The sentence seeps in and metabolises, fusing with my own thoughts and language.

ELLENA SAVAGE
BARE LIFE

Ellena Savage is the author of the
2020 essay collection *Blueberries*,
which was shortlisted for the
Victorian Premier's Literary Awards
and longlisted for the Stella Prize.

SIMÓN ENTERED MY ROOM and gave me a look. Unconsciously, and then consciously, I pressed my body into a pose, breasts forward, ass to one side, and lifted the sheet, an invitation that suggested this was how I always lay before 10 a.m., like a steamed clam.

Since we'd moved into the house on the island with many rooms, three or four months earlier, Simón and I luxuriated in the possibilities for privacy the rooms afforded – from one another, and from the world. Occupying separate bedrooms was intended to add a deeper texture to our lovemaking, because we would not, like other couples, stew in each other's farts each night, rather we would be independent creatures, with secrets. My secret was that I stared at my laptop screen until the early hours of the morning while time and my identity dissolved; but being a secret, it could have been anything. And so each morning Simón sauntered into my room; each morning we performed the same song and dance about the carnal ritual about to take place.

Lately though, I had begun to feel as if my body were a dying, drooping flower, turning away from the facts of life, from sun, from the hungry tickle of bees. I had heard of the affliction – bed death, libidinal annihilation – but I did not approve of the concept. I believed instead that if I forfeited my right to the physical pleasures – laying for hours in bed of an afternoon, the good parmesan, the sensation of a person's life rattling against your own with conviction – there would be no fixed reason for living. It *was* living. A body that folded up against its senses was as good as dead, and despite the sensory deprivations incurred by global health mandates, I was, it seemed, alive.

I believed then as I do now that there is no delineation

between a body and a life. The places where you found yourself, social places as well as those marked out in space and time, circumscribed who you were and what you could become; they set the furthest limits of your imagination. Your place determined your dreams, I thought, and I had begun dreaming about severed heads speaking to me from toilet bowls. I had been saying this for years, blood sack equals life! Space-time is a prison! But nobody listened. Granted, I had no audience to speak of. They – my non-audience, the world – seemed only to discover this humiliating truth, the truth of being sorely material and nothing else, when they, *their personal bodies,* were confined to a room, or two rooms. Only then did they concede that this might speak to a more general human condition. Ah ha! I said, to no one: How are your Eternal Forms going now? Now, individual bodies, i.e. people – i.e. ungovernable mysteries – had been rendered by the state as problems to be managed. To say I felt vindicated was an understatement. Yet my reward for vindication was the same as the punishment for those who had lived under delusions of the body's irrelevance: Internment. Boredom. Biopower.

This last term, biopower, is obviously not my own, though I am frequently perturbed at how marginal it has become even among the correctly paranoid leftists who constitute my milieu. Broadly speaking the concept appears in several politico-philosophical lineages; it describes the manner in which ordinary human life is subject to sovereign domination through regimes of population management. Biopower stretches from the overtly evil – eugenics, mandatory sterilisation, withholding abortion – to the more apparently 'neutral' – surveillance, genetic engineering, economically inscribed gender roles, universally mandated vaccines, and of course, lockdowns. One favourite iteration of the concept was in the work of a particular Italian philosopher, who made the case that biopower is used to create states of exception, wherein actual life and death is determined by the sovereign, acting well beyond law and reason. Ironically, the Italian philosopher appeared to lose his mind during his own subjection to the pandemic state of exception, and he left evidence of his unravelling in a belligerent personal blog. Simón and I were not having much sex by then, we had given up both watching television and drinking alcohol, and so there was little left to live for: we followed the Italian philosopher's blog closely. In his long and influential career, the Italian philosopher had argued that the story of Western civilisation was a story of the gradual and near-total diminishment of the status of human political life. Over time, he argued, the majority's tolerance towards the diminishment of abjected minorities became a tolerance for their own – the majority's – diminishment. For example, where once fingerprints had been used to control the criminalised underclasses, now everybody traded them with states to cross borders. The Italian philosopher had even cancelled a course he was scheduled to teach in the United States for this reason; he refused to give his fingerprints to the American government in order to enter the borders of the nation state. *Humanity itself,* he wrote, *has become the dangerous class.*

I appreciated a principled philosopher. It filled me with joy to imagine the old man stomping along in ugly pants at one of those aimless, exciting protests where violence occurred. Yes, oppressive technologies that were tested at the peripheries eventually came for the centre, like a virus. Césaire had said it.

Fanon had said it. Arendt, and Foucault. And now, here it was, it – biopolitical control under the guise of universal lockdown – had come for all of us, it had even come for Madonna. The Italian philosopher had called this diminishment of life to its essential ingredients – air and food, existence only – *bare life*, the condition of life stripped of specificity and particularity. This critical term, bare life, was usually deployed by PhD students who'd never had a job to talk about prisoners, stateless people, or comatose bodies on life support, but you could at a stretch apply it to us, the sexless locked-down. After all, we were no longer individuals free to waste our human potential on poor choices of our making; we were vectors forced to waste our lives only in state-sanctioned ways.

So far Simón and I were in agreement with the Italian philosopher. In one blog post, the philosopher discussed the story of Antigone, the Sophoclean tragic heroine who goes against the edict of her uncle Creon, the new ruler of Thebes, to bury her brother's body, who was murdered by Creon's own son. The play famously characterises the prohibition against Antigone burying her dead as a breach of divine law, and this is what the Italian philosopher was arguing too, that the prohibition during the pandemic lockdown against individuals burying their dead was a grave violation of their divine rights, a violation we were all casually allowing. I happened to agree with the Italian philosopher. Why were people encouraged to turn up to their workplaces, to risk ill health or even death merely to continue the rituals of trade, but they were forbidden from attending their own parents' funerals? This was the kind of decision that went against every edict of divine dignity. I was moved by this literary flourish in the Italian philosopher's blog post.

But where the Italian philosopher had once been a powerful writer who moved at rocket speed between philosophy, myth, literature and politics, the overall tenor of his blog posts more closely resembled polemics written by syndicated columnists with an axe to grind. Polemic was a form I found I could no longer tolerate, even when it was touched by the sun of intellectualism, as in the case of the Italian philosopher (who was in this regard following in the footsteps of another, Slovenian, philosopher I did not trust), still, it replicated the extremities of the rapacious mass media. The polemicist, I thought, shuts down reciprocity in favour of a banal and war-mongering monologue, and in doing this, he abolishes the other. Things took a bleak turn, then, when the Italian philosopher argued that anyone who agreed with the lockdown was like Eichmann.

Many saw this swerve as his fatal error.

This was also where Simón and I departed in our agreement. Simón believed the Italian philosopher had breached an ethical limit in invoking the Shoah so casually. In and of itself that's a serious error, he said, but what's worse is that he fed legitimacy to the neo-fascists who were using that very language to victimise themselves. The Italian philosopher, said Simón, is complicit in this appropriation, it's dangerous, and he's not even willing to acknowledge it. He's undermining his entire legacy.

I didn't disagree that the Italian philosopher was undermining his legacy with such fatuous claims, but on the other hand, I found it difficult to believe that people occupied the same planet that I did and were genuinely offended by obviously stupid, overreaching, ugly arguments. The world's largest economy, which described itself as the leading light of liberalism, was the biggest arms trader in history. The search engine that informed the global population on all matters of critical information was a gargantuan advertiser, which warped all data towards the object of infinite consumption. There were more enslaved workers on earth now than at any other time in human history, and the primary function of federal governments worldwide was to redirect the taxes paid by citizens to fossil fuel conglomerates while suppressing popular uprisings. The Mexican cartel death toll was in the six figures; celebrities and academics disappeared every day in China; entire small economies were wiped out by bonds traders placing bets to enhance their personal wealth. The Great Pacific Garbage Patch was now three times the size of France.

The scale is all off, I thought, almost out loud. The super-structure abounded with arguments so dull, so intentionally, blandly polarising they shut down any possibility for new, striking, beautiful ideas – that *was* the superstructure. Could anyone seriously read an argument that was incorrect, or even dangerous, and feel, genuinely feel, wronged to their core? Were they living in the same realm as me? Who was going to tell them? Were they going to be okay, once they knew?

In other words, I argued to Simón, I believed the argument's error was not moral – there was no such thing as pure morality, only material distributions that accrued ethical values by representing interests – but aesthetic. I did not want to be reminded of high school debating, was my point, which I had hated even in high school because it irritated my aristocratic senses. It was always false-naivety-this, pretend-outrage-that, and every argument always, without fail, ended up name-checking one murderous dictator or another. You had to be desperate and charmless to go there, I said to Simón, you had to be out of cards, you had to care for nothing but winning a limp little game. What's more you had to think your audience was too vain to notice. In other words, I said to Simón, you had to be fifteen to do any of this, but he was not fifteen, the Italian philosopher, he was seventy-eight years old. This kind of argument was the bare life equivalent of arguing, I argued; it was *bare text*, humourless cliché, it betrayed no investment in truth-seeking or meaning-making. It was a floppy, flaccid, stretched-out polyester, and it had no place in the life I was constructing, which was a beautiful artwork composed of richly dyed antique natural fibres that would last another century at least. It made me want to set myself on fire.

A stiletto of light stabbed through the badly hung sheet which I was using as a window covering, and got my eye. I moved my head to the side, and this action contorted my back into an even more seductive arch. I looked up at Simón's face and saw stars move across it. In a living argument against stark life, bare text, and the extinction of divine rights, I would have to stir myself to action, I thought. If I was to be consigned to the role of monitored, surveilled vector, at least I could refuse the ruin of my erogeneity. I opened the sheet even wider than it was before, and Simón slid in. He touched me in the usual, well-established ways, he nibbled my neck and breathed heavily and patted the outline of my body with his enormous, knuckly hands, and I licked his face fulsomely, though I did not enjoy it. He uttered the typical remarks, *so hot, so sexy, so hard, gunna fuck you*, and I didn't push him away, in fact I moved my body with his, to wake it up, though no whisper of reciprocation made itself known. We went on like this for a minute or two.

His lips came down on mine and I slid my face to one side. His large chest moved on top, squashing me, and the image that came to mind was of a large pile of dead cows from the mad cow epidemic of the early nineties. Grudgingly, I slow-danced with the motion. My hand, as was its habit, reached for his scrotum and let soft gravity do its work; as I cupped his testicles, tenderly, I avoided the shaft – somehow this felt chaste enough for my unstirred form. Simón was a hunk, literally, a large piece of something, ribs, mostly, and vascular enclaves, and his body had a nineteen-forties appeal. *Sailor,* I had almost said aloud when we first met: *Sailor, Simón, Sailor,* a prayer, knowing that the glamorous, homosexual aspect of the nautical professions had been made redundant by automation, just as Karl Marx had predicted (a sailor, like every other profession now, was a drone). When he stood tall, the breadth of Simón's ribcage made it appear as though he were sucking in his stomach, like a muscle man at the beach who was really just a thickset teenager. I refused to believe he did that on my account, sucked in his belly – the possibility of it gave me too much responsibility and I was overburdened as it was.

As Simón ground his large body on mine, I vaguely intuited the presence of my libido, despite myself; a small pearl hidden inside a rotten oyster at the bottom of the sea. It *was* there, that erotic ache that never really left, but it was distant, abstract, incredible. I could not reach it, could not crack open the shell and expose it to the light. Now, after several minutes of touching and moaning – his touch, his moans – I finally reached for his hand, which was squeezing my right buttock, placed it on my back, and ground my false-humping to a halt. Sorry, I said, sorry, sorry. I don't know. He sighed and rolled off me. I'll get coffee, said in a stiff little voice. He trotted out of my room, his cock a hot pink poker before him.

I knew I was allowed to *not* fornicate, I was a member of the enthusiastic consent sub-generation whose rule was that no one was to have any sex they did not rapturously, excessively, and verbally desire. But avoiding the act due to loss of libido by historical catastrophe was a sad rule. Carl Jung had defined libido as the totality of psychic energy, it was what animated a person, and he was not wrong. I didn't want impersonal history to leave its stench on my bedroom floor. In more immediate terms, I worried that if I didn't find a way back to my sexuality, and quickly, I would lose Simón. I did not have what anyone would call low self-esteem; no, I suffered from accurate self-estimation, a rare condition, and I therefore understood that Simón was the first person I'd been with who could do a lot better than me. Sexual enchantment was my one means of distracting a person from the glaring faults of my personality and the absence of my prospects. And I was intent on keeping Simón however long I could.

Before Simón, I had dated men involved in petty crime or who worked as security guards – often these were the same men. They had, my three main boyfriends, all been smart in the informally educated way; abreast of the news and aware of world events and sensitive to the systems that produced them, but with certain incorrect information going in that made things seem more organised than they really were. I shared some of their sensibilities, but even I had my limits. When Mikey the bass player slash weed dealer was stoned out of his mind, he would rant about the Illuminati, and this was not great. I had tried to dissuade him by telling him about the richest people I knew, the bankers and football players I served lobster platters to at my part-time horror job at Claws, the casino lobster house. Morons, I said. Incompetents. They pay hundreds a year to be part of the VIP club, I said, and all they get is a special lobster pick and a monogrammed bib! You can't entrust these oafs with running entire cabals. I have to tie their bibs round their necks, I said, stressing the point. They don't possess the power of their own extremities!

Incompetent, said Mikey; maybe. But powerful. Power isn't a result of competence, he said. If that were true, mothers would run the world. Power results from a willingness to violate others to advance one's own interests, he said, and I thought, Not bad. You could post that on Instagram. Mikey continued. We're not privy to their machinations, he said and then paused dramatically, sinking into his filthy sofa, his eyes glazed like marbles. Because we haven't been initiated into the paedophile death cult on Epstein Island.

In retrospect, Mikey had not been entirely wrong.

Liam and Jamal were not that far gone, but they were prone to saying things about 'the liberal media' and 'the Clintons', which could be embarrassing in bourgeois company but with which I more or less agreed. They'd all had aspirations, my boyfriends, but ordinary, achievable ones, like one day investing in real estate, or going back to school to do a business degree. Not ridiculous aspirations like winning the Nobel Prize for Literature, which Simón had never outright claimed to aspire to, but which I suspected he had considered at least once. With them, the exes, love had been a storm that raged inside me – I harboured for them obsessive, scandalous feelings which were known only to me, and then, as if spontaneously, I lost interest. I was careful to conceal these relationships from the authorities – God, accountants, and the king. These haphazard couplings were conducted under a cloud of secrecy, but I don't really know why. Was it because I was embarrassed by them? Or they by me? Whatever the reason, before Simón, I had never had any kind of relationship which expanded beyond the narrow confines of the bed. I had loved that kind of intimacy, which felt taboo. One layer of self-knowledge told me I was dirty and appalling, and falling in love with men who had no strong ties to the community and had considered careers in porn gave me a positive outlet for these feelings. We were dirty and appalling together, having crazy sex under the umbrella of the love god.

Simón was different. He had grown up largely in an outer western suburb after his parents' lives had been downgraded by their migration, not that they had been well-off in Belgrade. Yet somehow he had wrangled it such that he gave off serious upper-middle-class energy. He was what is called a good boy, gentle and extremely bright. He had gone to a suburban private school that preposterously called itself a Grammar on a scholarship, which was where, I supposed, he learned to conceal the nature of his situation – his bed a fold-out sofa in the living room of the one-bedroom he shared with his parents – not by dressing sharply and paying attention to personal grooming like the less socially attuned young men in his situation did; instead he established a toff-ish identity by dressing down, like the real sons of judges. He wore loose-fitting, worn-out linen shirts ('worn' because they were indeed second-hand) and raw calico shorts, he wore shoes without socks (I later learned that he wore ordinary socks but folded their cuffs over their gussets to disappear them). He wore his hair floppy and unkempt, suggestive of a person with distant but credible connections to one royal family or another, and he seemed always to be smiling to himself – one of the sexiest features in a man, indicating as it did that the smiler always knew what was going to happen next, and what would happen next would work out in his favour. It was a successful pose which eventually reified; if you insisted on a certain reality with the discipline of endless repetition, so it became.

Simón's attraction to me was therefore somewhat mysterious. I did not share with him the memory of bombs, or dislocated parents, nor the global variety of pecuniary distress, and yet I was not making use of the relatively ample resources available to me. Simón seemed to embody the desires for self-actualisation that liberal democracy had bequeathed to us all but which most of us were too lazy, too distracted, too self-delusional to action. Nobody so objectively desirable as Simón had ever chosen me, and so I consoled myself by imagining I possessed the qualities he projected onto me in order to pursue our relationship. The hopeful part of me imagined that Simón was simply a clear-sighted person who knew what he wanted and what he wanted was me, a 'real' person, with real love handles, real HECS debt for an unfinished degree, real dental neglect. But next to my hope I harboured a deeper, more intractable belief, which was that he chose me because I posed no threat to his accomplishments nor the unflinching confidence he needed in order to give to his work as much as he did.

And so it was crucial, I thought, despite the naked wishes of my biology, that I save my haunches with the trickery of sex.

Simón walked back into my room double fisting two mugs of black French press and I reached deep into myself to pluck the pearl from its hidden place. I shook my shoulders out, lifted my chin, and faced his body with mine.

HARALD VOETMANN
COMMON ROOM ROCKING HORSE

Translated by Johanne Sorgenfri Ottosen

Harald Voetmann is a Danish writer who has been nominated for the Nordic Council Literature Prize. He has written novels, short stories, poetry, and a monograph on the Roman poet Sulpicia. He also translates classical Latin literature, notably Petronius and Juvenal. *Awake*, the first in his series of three historical novels, was published in English in 2022.

Johanne Sorgenfri Ottosen is a Danish translator born in 1986. She currently lives in Copenhagen where she also works as an illustrator and literary editor.

SOMEONE DID GIVE BIRTH TO ME. Why remains unclear. Maybe they wanted to be loved, or it just sort of happened. It's unlikely they're alive. Then again, modern medicine. But so much time has passed since the fruitless event. The one who gave birth to me and the other, him, who may or may not have wanted something out of it other than to unload. And what exactly did *she* want. To be loved for it, or after it, to be loved by him, by me, by a third party. It's not unthinkable, though it does appear remote and foolish. Why did she grow me. From the moment they fished me out, I was never alone again, never again part of someone else. I sat there like an utterance, the answer to a question no one had asked or thought needed asking. With these saggy cheeks and dopey eyebrows. I am not suggesting anyone ever wished to give birth to something like me specifically. But it is a common assumption. Others suppose so when one walks by. Born after all, brought into being. It is what others assume. One doesn't even have to walk anywhere, one can sit, or not even that. Just being there, that's enough to make them come over and make assumptions. That someone willed you into the world. And the world will not leave you be. Not once you've been willed into it, or supposedly willed into it. Then they wrap you up in language and table manners to make it look like there's a purpose behind it all, like it's not just, not just nothing, nothing in the world, but a something which although neither imagined nor hoped for did sprout in someone's belly once, was fished out and given language and table manners. Wrapped in diapers so as not to sully the world, not toddle off and make it more sordid than necessary. And from then on never alone again, never again a part of someone. Which everybody was, beyond a doubt, at some point and this everybody does include me.

47

To lean back and forth on the common room rocking horse, thinking that I was part of something, a motion if nothing else, that might eclipse my pure presence for a moment. Pure, as in not part of anything; hardly counted, hardly desired, and if desired then not fitting. A useless spare part grown from a discontinued model as if of its own accord, which is precisely not the case. It's all very imprecise.

But on the rocking horse there were moments of oblivion, there was unity so to speak. The rocking horse had no purpose other than this: granting me escapes from my rather unique existence, or my utterly unique existence to be exact – unique though never alone, that is to say, uniquely futile, and only in futility ever truly alone – that was the purpose of the common room rocking horse. I rocked and I forgot a little and I forgot a little.

The rocking horse wasn't exclusively for toddlers. But apart from me only toddlers coveted it. Pulling a diapered kid down from it wasn't hard. Leaving it to wail on the floor, another chance to lose the sense of self. I rocked back and forth leaning against the horse's neck, sticking my index fingers through the hole that made up its eyes so that my fingertips met inside the horse's head, and I uttered a sound not entirely in tune with the little one's wail but more like an accompaniment, a singalong to the best of my ability.

The toddlers weren't the problem, although they did cause trouble whenever the adults grew tired of the racket. When a small one made too much noise one could sense our shared agenda: to be part of something larger, however insignificant the part and however meaningless the whole. And even if the crier only cried for himself, the crying was something to partake in, to dissolve into – dissolve into tears as they say, and I include myself among them, with their table manners and terms – even if I don't remember ever having let myself dissolve quite like that. Tears don't come easy, they never have. And when they do appear they don't act as a dissolvent. On the contrary, they seem to enhance the impression of something personal about me. And so he sits, dripping from under his heavy brows. But tears were something to envy if nothing else, and in this envy, partly dissolved by my rocking, the sound of crying was something to sing about.

It's reasonable to suspect that I was once a vessel of impersonal tears, a voice in the chorus of ear-splitting screams over having been put here. A scream not pertaining to this body. Nor whether anyone had wished for it or held any opinion regarding its birth. Or even entertained notions of being loved by it or being loved by a third party because of its excretion. I must have had the capacity, before everything else happened, to cry like that, dissolved, so that life itself could cry through me. Bullshit.

The problem was the big ones, same age or older, laden with notions of being someone, let loose in common space with kids to beat and objects to beat them with, a wish to overcome a certain measure of resistance. They were searching for a scoop of bravado in the horse riding tot they were punishing. Not only for the tot to fall off the rocking horse but to bleed a little maybe, maybe cry, and if so, cry feebly and softly. Without spirit or resistance, a cheapskate who won't share his pain.

One is forced to become someone because others feel that need. They need to distinguish themselves from relatable but more pitiful peers. Torn from the rocking horse myself, unable to cry about it in a meaningful way. Not meaningful, not becoming. Just a very personal whimper. Seems to bring out the porcine quality of the nose under the bulky brows, which hardly improves the design.

The dinner table provided another shot at self-oblivion, in the intake of sustenance, the act of mastication, the enforced quiet, the sight of the long, ungainly faces benched around the meal and asked to shut up, 'Chew! Silence! Table manners!' So that they could be all set and nourished for their continued gawking, wondering why the hell anyone would have wished to give birth to you at all. Their faces elongated with the chewing motions which took place under supervision though not exactly close supervision. The food had to be chewed properly, mashed to a slush, a gruel in the oral cavity, before further passage was granted to the boy's throat and on, to become harmlessly uniform chyme inside his gut. A shared dejection shone from the munching faces. Long, exposed and silent. Even the eyes were not merely wide open and distant, but stretched out too.

Such as that dog is, who by barking craves,
And quiet grows soon as his food he gnaws,
For to devour it he but thinks and struggles,
The like became those muzzles filth-begrimed...

How I relished those sessions. Here at last was community, in torpid melancholy, a half hour of forced brotherhood at the home.

Before and after the meal each face was like a fist, clenched around each seething will. Knuckle-eyes everywhere in common room and dormitory. In the dormitory, though, they could dissolve by other means. When they lay hissing and pulling, fists clenched around their pee-pees. What took place here was not an elongation but a further clenching of the faces. Knuckle-eyes straining to white until sort of busting, legs twitching and toes kneading the collectively farted up air. Even though they did it together – simultaneously, I mean – it was not a shared experience but a highly individual fade or retreat to an overarching community, vaguely discernible in the gleam across their spasmodic faces or as echoing faintly in their grunts.

At least I recognised here the urge to disappear into something, and when they lay limp and spent, striped with seminal fluid down the front of their pajamas, a calm descended not unlike the one imposed by 'Silence! Table manners!' Where there is no true community to be had one may still find something recognisable, and this includes me too.

Then came other journeys, the same rocking back and forth turned to propulsion, or an aimless drift into the world at least. People needed to see my ticket, stamp my passport, rummage through my bag. Most acted as though my drift had a purpose. The fields were green and golden streaks smeared along my vision. On occasion: a mountain, an inlet, a high-rise. Clouds and the chimneys of incineration plants. Some things appeared to stand still and not blur completely into motion. I collected the moments: the trembling nostrils of a fellow passenger. An old woman in the seat across from mine, offering me a pastille from a pretty antique tin. Or maybe she didn't. But there was a delightful creak when she opened and closed the lid of her ornate reliquary for one of the ancient goodies. That she could resist the temptation to do it constantly. Creak, creak, I heard the sound only once through the entire trip but I've kept it ever since.

Hours on platforms and in waiting rooms. To be waiting is to be something. Awaiting the motion itself as well as to be part of it, a presence subject to a purpose. Compartments heavy with human smells, thickened by the toilets around us. Our sweat glands, rotting teeth and dirty rectums.

We were in the stench together, surely – the blurred beauty of the landscapes may not have registered with everybody, but the stench must have, we created and perceived it together and I was certainly a part of that too.

Only the rocking horse's eyes were free of hate. Technically, it was one eye, a hole drilled through its head, all the way through the slab of wood. Round and empty, unity and absence combined. If one was to imagine its perspective, what that tunnel saw, it must have been a gaze unfamiliar with the outer world, instead turned inward from either side, meeting itself somewhere around the center. A determined withdrawal, unlike my own scattered attempts at dissolution. No knuckle-eyes could ever meet that gaze.

It was impossible to see both sides of the hole at once. Viewed frontally, only its slant forehead and the ragged leather remaining of its left ear could be seen – the right ear was long eroded by toddlers' chewing and fondling. No eyes were indicated at all from the front. Kneeling by the animal's flank, staring through the hole, one's vision vanished inside the animal and came back on the other side. The evasion was total and admirable. Contact was impossible and yet the gaze was comforting. Sitting on the common room rocking horse, I leaned forward and vanished a bit in its rocking, forgot a little. From each side I stuck my fingers inside the eyehole. Where the fingertips met we were together.

KAT CAPEL
SIGHTSEEING

Kat Capel is a writer of fiction and poetry. They grew up living in Castlemaine on Dja Dja Wurrung land, in the small town of Tennant Creek on Warumungu country, and in Cairns, also known as Gimuy. Their first book of poetry, *Work & Love*, was published by Incendium Radical Library in 2021 and was highly commended for the Deakin University Nonfiction Prize. Kat is also currently a PhD candidate at RMIT University. They are working on their first novel from their home on Wurundjeri country in North Melbourne.

THE HOUSE HAD BRICKS the colour of runny shit and a linoleum floor that was so thin you could scrape a hole in it by pushing back your chair. When Michael arrived, his father was talking on the phone in the kitchen while stirring something on the stove. There was no smell that Michael could distinguish. Not for the first time in his life he felt glad for his father's interiority. Most likely he would not ask Michael too many questions, or object when Michael managed to avoid answering them.

He unpacked the car by himself, piling all of his belongings up against the far wall in the spare room that his father insisted on calling his office. On the desk there was a piece of paper that had some kind of mind map drawn on it. There was a word in the middle that was circled and then smaller words that branched off it with lines zigzagging in between them in all directions. His body grew warm and excited. He liked private things, it didn't matter what. But then of course, he thought about Briohny and Lila and Jan. He refrained from taking a closer look. Instead he went and had a shower, and then began packing clothes into an orange carry-on suitcase he had found in the spare room cupboard.

The next day they arrived at the airport at 7.15 a.m. Michael was to board a plane to Auckland. He would have a layover there for seven hours before boarding another plane to Guangzhou, where he would stay with his friend Adam. As his father prepared to pull away he wound down the window and said something, but Michael couldn't hear.

'What?'

His father spoke again, but again he couldn't hear. Annoyed, Michael shuffled closer to the car, his large backpack swinging violently from one shoulder. As he approached he saw that a worried look had come over his father's face.

But 'fly safe' was all he said.

'I will,' Michael smiled, and then he turned his back on his father and the car and headed for the escalator that led down towards the terminals.

It was October 2019, and having suddenly found himself with no rent to pay, no household responsibilities, no pets or dependants, he felt a holiday spirit overcome him. He felt the rush of excitement that came from being cut loose. He felt his grip on the routine of his life slacken, as a person might relax their hold on the leash of a child in a shopping centre. It is this kind of promise that puts people on planes, that causes even the most environmentally conscious among us to forget ourselves.

He had sent Adam a text message two days ago saying that he had spontaneously decided to spend three weeks in China, and could he possibly stay a few nights with him in Guangzhou. To his relief, Adam had replied some hours later saying that he was welcome to stay. Other than his cousin who was at a dance school in London, Adam was the only person Michael knew who lived in another country.

Unfortunately, because it had been booked just the day before, the flight had cost a lot: $3,680 Australian dollars. He had also paid $109.99 online for a thirty-day Chinese tourist visa, which had arrived in just six hours as promised. Luckily, these purchases made only a small dent in his savings. He had spent the past three years working four days a week at Royal Park in inner city Melbourne. The job paid a slightly-above-minimum wage that he was often too tired to spend, and that had therefore accumulated. It consisted of weeding, spraying pesticides and cutting down dangerous tree branches with a chainsaw so that they didn't fall on the people who frequented the park.

In summer sweat rolled down his arms and pooled into the fingertips of his rubber gloves, and he came home with a rash on the inside of his thighs. Often the park became populated with groups of people he knew, but who often didn't recognise him in his high-vis clothing and wide-brimmed hat. In fact they rarely ever seemed to see him at all, as though he were simply part of the landscape.

In the line for security he realised he had forgotten to empty out his water bottle. Rather than lose his place, he chugged down the entire litre in lengthy bursts, pushing his carry-on suitcase forwards with his foot as he went. It was 7.34 a.m. By now, Briohny would already be at work, and Lila and Jan would almost definitely still be sleeping. He wondered if they were happy, now that he was gone.

Michael had met Adam at university in a class called 'Queer and Feminist Perspectives'. Adam was intelligent and gentle. He was inclusive. He was popular with their female peers. When he came over to Michael's house, the five of them would often cook and eat together. Adam was Greek and lived with his parents in a big house in Northcote that had exposed timber beams on the roof and slate floors. They were relaxed and never minded that the two of them sometimes spent entire days there hungover or coming down from drugs. Michael and Adam would order pizza and eat it sprawled on the floor of the room the family called 'the TV room', the only room that had carpet, with their shirts discarded on the couch.

Throughout the duration of his undergraduate degree he worked at the same place, and lived with the same people, Briohny, Lila and Jan, with the same work-related rash, year after year. Whenever he wondered if he was happy he concluded that yes, he was, since there was nothing he could think of that he would change. Adam, in comparison, was like a mathematician. He approached his life like that, always adding and removing. In this way he always had what he perceived to be the best of things. He went through four different jobs: a Mauritian fine-dining restaurant, a call centre, the reception desk of a doctors' office, a not-for-profit encouraging artistic development in young people. He went on frequent and well-planned overseas holidays, travelling through Indonesia, Malaysia, Vietnam and Thailand, and then Hungary, Poland, Romania and Ukraine. When he travelled he always sent Michael postcards, which Michael read and stuck to the fridge with magnets.

There was something about Adam that made Michael feel like he could tell him things, even bad things about himself, and that he wouldn't mind. He sometimes fantasised about writing him a letter, a long letter where he confessed everything, a letter where he left nothing out. He never did, but the fact remained that Adam seemed to exude a sense of approval towards him that he didn't understand but that he needed, and therefore latched onto. Then, in 2018, Adam said he was moving to China permanently for a job in the philanthropy sector. It was around this period of time, perhaps even that very night, that they had sex. Michael remembered that in the hours beforehand they had both kept crossing and then uncrossing their legs. In bed Adam had been cautious with his touches, as though Michael's body was a dangerous thing, or else vulnerable to breaking. Alternately, Michael did it like he would with anyone.

When they saw each other next, at a pub everybody went to near the uni to talk about philosophy or else just to drink, it was clear in the way that Adam pulled out his chair, in the way that he poured his water, in the particular way he asked Michael if he wanted anything from the bar, that it would never happen again. Michael didn't mind. He knew that Adam was mostly straight. Besides, Michael didn't really like having sex. For him it had been done experimentally, to see how they, as two people, fit together. This was something he thought about a lot. The idea that there was something particular about their friendship that even fucking couldn't solve.

When Adam picked him up from the Guangzhou airport however, he smiled weakly, and took Michael's backpack and put it in the car without embracing him, as if he were in a rush. Michael noticed straight away that Adam looked very different. His dark curls had been cut short and bleached blonde. He had a deep crease on his forehead that, if it wasn't a wrinkle yet, soon would be. Where Michael's own signs of ageing were primarily located in the corners of his eyes, from squinting into the sun or else through darkness, Adam had told him on one of their phone calls that he spent all day staring at a computer, and that despite the blue-light-blocking glasses he wore he often found himself with a headache that caused him to frown. As Adam drove, his hands kept kneading the rubber on the wheel, which made a strange squelching sound. His forearms were bigger than they had been, at least four times the width of his wrist. He was older, Michael realised. They both were. Older and bigger. His own stomach strained against the seatbelt.

Through the window, clusters of mid-rise buildings floated by, surrounded by greenery that he did not recognise. Sheets and T-shirts dripped from balconies. It was raining, a fine mist that glittered this way and that like static. It hadn't occurred to

Michael to think about the weather. Places he hadn't been to existed in a weatherless state, except for those he had seen on the news flooded, crumbling or alight. For perhaps the first time he understood why people connected a change in environment with a change in spirit, psyche or self. It was easy to pretend for a moment that the person he was before, in Melbourne, and the person he was now, in Guangzhou, were different.

'Does it rain here all the time in summer?' he asked.

Adam kneaded the wheel again, producing the longest squelch yet. He thought for a while, as though Michael's question were somehow a deeply existential one.

'Nah, not really.'

That evening they ate at a restaurant that had two menus, one written in Chinese characters and one full of pictures of meals which had correlating numbers. Michael noticed the picture menu was quite short, and only contained things he had tried before, like eggplant with garlic sauce or pork belly. He wanted to try something more exciting.

'Sure, let me just send this message,' Adam said, not looking at him but typing something on his phone.

'Work?' Michael asked.

Adam ignored him. He typed furiously and for a long time, his eyebrows and lips clumped together. Michael waited patiently. The restaurant was dim. It had several large windows that were tinted, which made the busy street outside look mysterious and unknown. It seemed that all of the people who flashed by were on their way to do something uncouth. He dragged his gaze away from the windows and studied his fellow diners. There was nobody in particular that intrigued him. Everybody except them was Chinese. They all had their food already, and were eating. Only the young girl who kept coming out onto the floor in order to clear dishes had anything interesting about her. She had an unnerving habit of whipping her hair back over her shoulder with an aggressive snap of her neck. She was not particularly attractive, and yet like most teenagers there was something compelling about her. When she wasn't whirling around the room snatching plates and bowls off tables, she stood slumped in various locations staring glassily at her phone, which made him want to know what exactly she was looking at.

Michael tore his attention away and scrutinised the characters on the pages of the menu. They were abstract and complicated. He tried to discern a pattern between them but found he could not.

After what must have been ten minutes or longer Adam put his phone down and ordered quickly in Mandarin. He poured them some tea. He sighed. He sighed again. He wiped some sweat from his face with his T-shirt, revealing the soft torso underneath. The hair there was still dark, twirling coarsely down his stomach into his cotton shorts like the roots of a vine. Michael fantasised about reaching out and giving it a good tug. He didn't, though. Like so many other things, the thought was more pleasurable than the act.

'Jan told me what you've been doing,' Adam said finally.

There was a silence where neither of them spoke. Michael noticed there was a small television screen mounted to the distant wall directly behind Adam, but it was so far away that he couldn't quite make out what was playing on it. He squinted. Colourful shapes moved around. They could have been people, or animals, or anything really.

Adam looked like he wanted to say something else, but at this moment the food arrived. Michael couldn't wait to put salt all over everything. There was a stir-fried plate of celery, carrot and snow peas, a small bowl of rice, four tiny translucent shrimp dumplings, two cups of something that looked like coffee but which jiggled when they were set down on the table, and most impressive of all, a whole piglet that sat splayed on all fours on an oval-shaped plate. The pig's ears were pricked up, as though it was listening. It was a beautiful golden colour, like autumn leaves.

Michael pictured his housemates the way they had been before he had left: Briohny in the cat's armchair, Lila sitting upright on one end of the couch wearing her cream corduroy skirt, and Jan at the hem, her knees tucked up to her chest. He had noticed that as the talking went on their bodies had leaned towards one another more and more, as if closing off the square to make it a triangle. He had heard somewhere that the human body actually had a large hole going right through the middle. He didn't know what that meant, but at this moment he had imagined that his was tubular and wet, like the throat of some hungry creature, or else like the engine of a car, which he imagined was somewhat hollow. Jan had been angry. Briohny and Lila had been sad. But the hole had swallowed up his apology like it was nothing more than a tiny, winged insect gone astray. He had not said sorry. Instead, he had stared at Jan's feet, which had rested flat on the cool tiles in front of him. Where the ends of Michael's own toenails peeled or flaked off before they could grow past the length of his actual toe, Jan's adorned the tips of her toes like baubles, like petals, like tiny alabaster pearls.

'If you knew why did you let me come?' he asked.

Adam glanced at him, then looked away.

'Because. I don't know.'

Michael wondered how much Adam knew, and then what version of the story he had been told. He knew Adam and Lila kept in touch because sometimes Lila came into the kitchen and recited something silly Adam had said to her or posted on the internet. It was obvious that she had a crush on him. It hadn't occurred to him though that Lila, that any of them, would go out of her way to tell anybody. Ironically, he had thought it was private. It wasn't that there was judgement in Adam's voice exactly. Worse. It was something closer to disappointment.

He looked down at the fork that the waiter had placed in front of him in lieu of chopsticks. For a moment he felt regret. Guangzhou was big and wet and unknown, but somehow, the world itself still felt suffocatingly narrow.

The next afternoon Adam had to work, so Michael was left in the apartment by himself. He went out through the glass door and stood on the small balcony. Nestled low down, between the colourful buildings that mushroomed across and up in all directions, he could see a flat bitumen area where he was astonished to see that children were practising marching. The movements were repetitive and familiar. He watched with dwindling interest. He knew he should go out and explore the city, but he found now that he was here some urgency had gone out of the whole thing. Suddenly the notion of travel and everything that came along with it felt banal and tiresome.

He had been especially interested in visiting the orchid garden, which had over two hundred varieties of the plant. His plan had been to go around looking at the orchids and then to drink tea in one of the many tea rooms that were there. Instead, he just went back inside and sat at the small circular dining table and stared at the framed poster of *The Beguiled* that hung behind the couch. The lounge had doors leading off to the spare room, which he had slept in, and to Adam's bedroom, the door of which was firmly closed.

The thing about doing something wrong was that, in adult life, there was very rarely anybody to catch you. There was law enforcement, but they were stupid and slow and would never notice someone like Michael, who was a young white man of slightly below average size in all directions. There were everyday citizens too, some of whom noticed things they shouldn't. Their pace would slow, their eyes would narrow, and then he'd have to do something like pretend he was looking for a ball or gardening. More often than not, there was nobody around at all, like now, although there were the three women on the poster of *The Beguiled,* one of whom seemed to watch as he slid, in nothing but his boxers and socks, towards Adam's bedroom door.

Inside Adam's room were the usual things: a bed, a desk, and a wardrobe. All of the furniture was made of the same cheap white chipboard, and though the room was sufficiently lived in (a pair of socks on the floor, an unmade bed, bills on the desk) everything was too empty. It seemed the poster in the other room was the only artwork in the whole apartment, and there were no photographs or mementos on the desk or bedside tables. It was very different from Adam's room back at his family home, which had been studded with posters of bands and sport memorabilia, and which had a cork board above the desk to which pictures of various friends and girlfriends were pinned. This room could belong to any single man, Michael thought, but then he opened the wardrobe and was surprised to see not only men's clothing but a yellow dress, several pairs of women's pants, a blouse. He lifted the bottom of the blouse to his nose and took a deep sniff. The smell of jasmine, or perhaps rose, filled his nostrils. He had always found it hard to tell the difference between floral scents. Jan had once tried to teach him, wrapping her hand over his eyes and holding up this flower or that. On that particular afternoon they had been bored, and so she had taken her clothes off and posed for him so that he could draw her, so easy and comfortable things had been between them. Now he took the blouse and lay down on the bed, enjoying the light weight of it draping across his shoulders, the cheap sheets scratching against his bare back.

Other people's interests usually involved buying or producing things, or going to special places, or using particular modes of transport, or playing games. These were called 'hobbies'. In contrast, he produced nothing. He consumed nothing. He experienced only what was already there, and left no trace. He was not in competition with anybody, in fact he took the greatest care not to involve anyone but himself. When successful, he made nothing happen, and affected nobody. Of course he knew the other difference was that hobbies often involved other consenting parties. In contrast, he asked for no permission, and even hid his actions. When unsuccessful, as he had been, he made everything happen, and affected everybody. In this way he consumed everything, and in doing so he produced it and took it for his own.

The first time he had done it, he'd scaled the brick wall at the back of the garden and, sitting atop it like a large hairless house cat, had looked straight into the next-door lounge room, where his neighbour was teaching her young daughter to play the guitar. The tips of the little girl's fingers were so small and fat across the strings that they resembled black jellybeans. As he watched he had noticed that, unlike with characters on television, he sometimes laughed when they laughed. The experience felt so pure, so nice, that he did it again. And then he did it again. It was mostly boring stuff that he saw; lonely boomers in nice houses watching television, teens scrolling on their phones, exchange students preparing toast or noodles. Most people were cliches of themselves, especially his housemates, who listened to Lana Del Rey while getting dressed, and ate in bed.

He began returning to his favourite spots not only at night but even in the middle of the day, if the mood struck. He took to leaving an ashtray and a bottle of water up on the wall, for example, so that he could smoke, which gave him his excuse to be out there. Lila saw him sitting there several times, but she just sat down at the janky courtyard table and complained about her ex-girlfriend, who she thought had prematurely started a relationship with somebody else. Michael didn't know whether this was true or not. He did know that Lila had sometimes treated the ex badly, because without even needing to spy he had watched her do it, in front of everybody in the kitchen. He also knew Lila had unrealistic ideas about love because of the uncommonly close relationship her parents had with one another, something he knew about in detail from reading their old letters, which he had found in a garish velvet box in the middle drawer of her desk.

The memory of finding and then opening the box sent a rush of blood to his penis, and he slipped his hand beneath his waistband and gripped. This memory was replaced by another, and then another as he lay there beneath the blouse, until what he saw became the indistinguishable concoction of reality and fantasy, of attraction and repulsion, that he required to come. Briohny was masturbating next to the velvet box. His own father was on all fours, his ass in the air. Appalled, he swiftly replaced his father with Adam, who was in missionary with a faceless but naked woman with a snatched waist and unreasonably gigantic tits. And then she wasn't naked but was instead wearing the blouse, stretched too tight over her bosom. And then Adam was wearing the blouse as he fucked her, and then for some reason there was another person there too, a man Michael had let fuck him once who had lived in Altona North and smelled like dishwashing liquid. The images went on until he finally finished, and then they abruptly but very naturally dulled and slipped away.

How did he understand his own behaviour? He felt a pressure to understand it. He felt that if he tried, he could put it into a narrative that forced it to make sense. But then he'd always found the optics of immorality arbitrary. Maybe he just wasn't thinking when he poked around in his housemate's rooms or peeped through their windows. But he knew this wasn't true. He had thought about it a lot, he was so overcome by self-interest.

It was only on his way out, having cleaned himself up with a tissue from the bedside table and returned the blouse, that he noticed the tennis ball sitting a metre or so away from the door. If he didn't know this trick he wouldn't have thought anything of it, but as it was he was familiar with this tactic. A suspicious person might put such an object up against the inside of the door so as to be alerted were it to be opened in their absence. It occurred to Michael, as he stared down at the ball, that his relationship with Adam didn't have trust, or honesty, or open communication, or anything else that a friendship was probably supposed to have. But then what did it have? He thought that the tennis ball seemed to point towards the answer. Maybe it wasn't approval, like he had once thought, but acceptance. Adam didn't mind if Michael snooped, he just wanted to know if, and when, he did. In this case he wondered what, if anything, would happen if he just left the ball where it sat, near the foot of the bed.

When Adam came home the two of them drank beer on the balcony and Michael talked about how his job at the park was going. Still, Adam did not mention a girlfriend or any female friends who might explain why he had women's clothes inside his wardrobe, and Michael did not let on that he had seen them.

That evening they went out to meet some of Adam's co-workers at a karaoke bar. The bar was small with intense purple lighting. They were the only ones there. There was a gigantic screen which played songs automatically if none were chosen. It faced a large, white couch in the shape of a crescent moon. Nobody except Adam seemed very interested in doing karaoke. Every time he recognised a song he leapt up and sang into the tinny microphone that was taped to its stand with shiny silver tape.

After a particularly enthusiastic rendition of 'I Gotta Feeling' by the Black Eyed Peas, Adam flopped down beside Michael and embraced him. He was noticeably more relaxed than he had been the previous day, and Michael wondered if this was because his stay was already coming to its end. The day after tomorrow he would commute to the nearby Baiyun Mountain, also known as White Cloud Mountain, where he would be able to see a view of the entire city from up in the clouds. Afterwards he would come back down and take a train to Shanghai. But there was something else that was different about Adam, a strange sadness in the way he held him. Had he put the tennis ball back? He realised with a thrill that he couldn't remember. Heat spread rash-like across Michael's body, especially his hands, which were folded limply around Adam's shoulder blades. But a moment later Adam had released him and was up and moving again, heading to the bar in a kind of uncoordinated shimmying walk dance, and the feeling subsided. Michael took a Wet Pussy shot from a tray on the table and downed it. Predictably, it tasted like cordial. He had another.

Adam's co-workers were all Chinese and male. They were from places Michael had never heard of and couldn't retain, the sounds were so unrecognisable. They asked Michael friendly questions about himself, fetched him more drinks and slapped him on the back. They seemed like the kind of people who would work in philanthropy. He mostly talked to a man called Tao, who it turned out was Adam's boss. Tao was the only one in the group who was from Guangzhou. He was talking a lot, explaining place names and giving directions and advice. He took Michael's phone and began writing down a long list of restaurants and things to sightsee. Go here, don't go here, take this bus, etc. Michael tried to listen, but he couldn't help noticing that when he wasn't singing, Adam kept putting his hand on the leg of one particular man who was often sitting next to him. If the man didn't like it, he didn't show it.

'There's this really funny place there actually,' Tao was saying, his thumbs flying excitedly across the screen.

'Yeah?' mumbled Michael, watching the door to the men's room swing closed behind Adam and the man.

'Yeah, it's this restaurant that's split into two venues. I guess it got really popular, so they expanded into the building next door. Anyway, between the two restaurants is this gap. I guess the people who built it made a mistake because they could have just made the buildings with a shared wall, instead of leaving a gap. But I guess they did it for some reason that we don't know. Everyone says if you can make it through the gap to the other side you'll have good sex for the next ten years!'

Suddenly irritated by Tao's continued use of the phrase 'I guess', he excused himself and went to the bar to pour himself a glass of water from one of the bottles there. As he drank the water, Michael realised he really was very intoxicated. He took his water back to the couch and sat down, feeling dizzy and nauseous. When Adam returned with the man, he was noticeably subdued. He plopped down on the couch close to Michael and looked at him blurrily, with the half-closed look of a drunk.

His head lolled backwards, exposing his throat. Michael looked at the man, who was seated next to Adam with his phone lit up in his hand. The man must have felt him looking, because he put his phone in his lap and swept his eyes lazily upwards until they landed on Michael. His gaze was cool and slick like butter. It went on for too long. The music was too loud. Michael imagined he could smell the man, but when he took another whiff he could only smell Adam's hoppy breath. His face was tilted towards him now, his mouth agape and his eyes closed as though waiting for a morsel of food.

It was still night when Michael woke up and ran to the toilet. He retched, but nothing came out. He sank down to the bathroom floor and stared at his phone. He had not realised he had taken it with him.

Jan picked up on one of the first few rings.

'Hello?'

He launched in.

'There's this place in a town near here – actually it made me think of you and that time you got stuck on that fence when we were leaving that rave. I don't know. I don't know what I'm saying,' he said, faltering.

'I'm in China,' he added, as if that would somehow communicate what he couldn't.

'You know Adam isn't gay, don't you? Not in the way you want him to be,' she said.

Jan sounded tired, and Michael realised that he had no idea what time it was in Australia. He felt sorry for her. How badly she had misconstrued the situation. How badly she had misread him. How terrible she was at uncovering the truth. He almost laughed out loud.

'I don't want to be with Adam, Jan,' he said, trying to control his glee.

'So why the fuck are you visiting him? What is he, like, your *best friend*?'

Still smiling, he shook his head, though of course Jan couldn't see this.

'No, you want him to be like you. You want him to make you feel like you've done nothing wrong. He's nice. He'll make you feel good. But–he's–not–like–you–Michael!' she said each word like she was hammering in a tent pole.

'He's cheating on his girlfriend. With a male co-worker.'

He was fishing. There was a pause.

'I seriously doubt that. They're engaged,' she said finally, as though this made all the difference.

There was another long silence.

It had been dark outside in Melbourne, darker than it could ever be in a megacity such as Guangzhou, and Jan's venetian blinds had been half drawn up, askew because they were broken. The window had been thrown open, and he had been able to silently climb out his own adjacent window and sidle down the side of the house against the fence until he was directly below it. Very slowly he had raised his head so that the crown, and then the forehead, then his eyes were above the windowsill. To make his crouching stance easier he had rested the tips of all ten of his fingers on the sill and gripped. He had been able not only to see her, but also to experience the smells and sounds of her being there. She had been lying on her bed playing a game on her phone. She played with the volume on loud, so that cute mechanical sounds bounced around between them. She had an oil diffuser lit that smelled like it had burnt dry. He had told himself he would leave soon. He had been breathing quite loudly through his nose, but just as he made to rectify this by opening his mouth he had felt something shift, and then Jan had looked up from her phone and straight at him. Only then did he realise she was naked.

It was physical, the way everything had twisted. He had felt the opening of some telepathic channel, as though suddenly Jan knew everything he had ever done or even thought about doing. Even his ears had tickled slightly, as though there was something or somebody reaching right into his ear canal. In this way he had felt things ring out, like a wet sheet held between two people who were turning it in very tightly in opposite directions in order to extract the moisture.

'Are you ever going to say sorry, Michael?' she asked now.

Her voice sounded funny. He realised that she was crying. Mechanically, he pulled the phone away from his ear and hung up.

He found that he was standing outside Adam's room. Gripping the door handle firmly, he very carefully turned the knob and pushed it open a few centimetres. Through the crack he could just make out Adam, naked and tangled in the sheets, his penis uncovered. As Michael edged into the room he was surprised to see that beside Adam there lay the body of a woman. Her face was turned away from him, but he could see that she was wearing earplugs and an eye mask. There was a suitcase in the corner of the room. It was not that he was surprised to see the woman so much as that he was surprised at what seeing the woman made him feel. He felt sad.

Adam and the woman had been sleeping facing one another with their knees touching, but as Michael watched, Adam rolled over, scooting his backside into the curve of the woman's body. She responded by wrapping her right arm around his waist. Michael half fell, half sat on the edge of their bed. Tears of his own ran down his cheeks and into the collar of the shirt that he had worn the night before and not taken off before falling asleep. It stank. He even hoped that they might wake up and find him there, but they slept on.

After a while his breathing slowed and he left the room and went out onto the balcony. Maybe it had been too easy to separate things from people, and people from things, he thought, staring out across the way into the block directly opposite. Just one apartment had its lights on, and he stared into their bleak lounge room, which had nothing but a grey couch and bike leaned up against the wall. Ultimately he didn't believe that people really cared about privacy – not really. People made a song and dance about it, but everybody told their secrets to at least one person. They put them online. They showcased them in the posters they put up and the jobs that they chose. They left them in diaries for him – for anybody – to find. This was one of the things that had drawn him to working with plants and animals, he realised. He liked being outside, where secrets were plentiful. Overhead there were no stars and no moon. No planes or satellites blinked down at him. The sky was blanketed by smog. It gave nothing away.

LIN BAI
THE LIGHT IN THE MIRROR

Translated by Nicky Harman

Lin Bai was born in Guangxi Province in 1958 and graduated in library sciences at Wuhan University. She worked as a librarian, a reader for a state film studio and a newspaper journalist, before beginning to write full-time. She has nine novels, as well as novellas, short stories, essays, and collections of poetry to her credit. Her 1994 novel, *A War of One's Own*, from which this piece is drawn, was an instant success and established her as a pioneer of women's literature in China. In 2013, her latest novel, *The Chronicle of My life in the North*, won the prestigious Lao She Literature Prize. She lives in Beijing.

Nicky Harman is a freelance literary translator from Chinese. When not translating, she works on Paper-Republic.org, a non-profit website promoting Chinese literature in translation, where she is also a trustee. She organises translation-focused events, mentors new translators, teaches translation summer schools and judges translation competitions. In 2020, she won the Special Book Award of China. Her most recent translation publication is *The Shaanxi Opera* by Jia Pingwa, co-translated with Dylan Levi King.

THIS LOOKING AT MYSELF, touching myself, it all started a long time ago. In nursery school, in fact, when I was five or six years old.

I knew that I shouldn't let anyone see, that it was something bad. Whenever the *ayi*, the careworker who patrolled the dormitory, was about to reach my bed, I forced myself to keep still, shut my eyes and pretend to be asleep as soon as I heard her footsteps.

I wanted to do it all the time. On long summer afternoons, we napped without the mosquito nets down so there was nothing to hide one bed from the next and the *ayi* had an unimpeded view of the whole room. But I would wait patiently until everyone had dropped off, the *ayi* last of all, and then I could relax and start doing it.

The *ayi*'s bed was by the window, several cots away from mine. I would lie there looking at it – it was bigger and slightly higher than ours – and what I could see of her, sometimes a long top and trousers, or a silky garment in pale blue or black, or white with short sleeves and flowers embroidered across the front.

The summer afternoons were hot and sticky. The cicadas chirped, but the rest of us were weighed down, suffocated, by the heat. If Mrs Huang was the *ayi* on duty I didn't need to worry. She was short-sighted and didn't wear glasses, just screwed up her eyes when she looked at you. She never scolded or made a fuss either. The stifling air filled the dormitory, gluing us to our beds. It felt like water, buoying me up so I floated.

The light was fierce in the afternoon. Even with my eyes shut, I felt naked and exposed. In the neighbouring cots, children tossed and turned or ground their teeth, and footsteps clomped loudly up and down outside. It was hopeless, I couldn't enjoy my siesta.

The night came.

We played games in the evening, then went to the classroom, where we sat on low chairs. They were pale green, and there were no tables. The teachers told us stories, or we sang songs or guessed riddles. Then there were snacks. I wasn't a greedy child but I always ate what I was given. Sometimes it was a couple of bayberries, or fruit drops, or a kind of banana, bigger than an ordinary banana, smaller than a plantain. They were called Saigon bananas though I don't know what they had to do with Saigon. Or sometimes we got a star fruit or a guava or, best of all, lychees. These grew abundantly where we lived. Most nights it was papaya, orange-coloured with sweet dense flesh, and seeds like black agate. The papaya trees were fantastically shaped, truly beautiful subtropical fruit trees. The fruit was sliced into segments and we took one each. Then we queued to wash our hands and queued to pee: we had to put our hands on the shoulders of the child in front so we formed a train, and make hooting noises as we moved forward. The train moved from the row of basins to the toilets, and from there to the dormitory. A teacher stood at the door, putting her hand on each child's forehead as we passed by her. (Fevers were a frequent occurrence.) We filed silently into the dorm, took off our shoes and lay on our cots. The *ayi* reached up and poked each mosquito net so that it dropped. Now we each had our own little room. No one could come in, and when the lights went out and the walls solidified, no one could see in either. I could do what I wanted. I turned myself into water and my hand into a fish, and it slid all over me, and so long as I made no noise, no one would come near.

I've carried on doing it like that, right up until now. For years, the mosquito net has been my partner in crime. Only a mosquito net keeps other people out and me safe inside.

I've always liked mirrors, I've always liked looking into secret places. During the long summers, alone in the shower room, I would spend ages looking at myself and stroking my body. At the age of eight, I discovered something hard in my left breast. My mother took me to see the medical team from Beijing who were working in the commune health centre. I sat on the back carrier of her bicycle and we pedalled from B Township to Xinxu, fifteen *li* with the sun beating down on our heads. This team were the experts, my mother said, and their Mandarin accents certainly sounded authoritative. They were friendly and kind too. After they had examined me, we went back to my mother's workplace, the county hospital, to pick up the medicines from the pharmacy. The walls were lined with bottles, filled with multicoloured liquids and tablets, and boxes. The medicines had a special good, clean smell that lingered on my mother's clothes and in her hair. My medicine was mixed from several large bottles, some with clear liquid in them, and others with cloudy liquid and a white sediment at the bottom. When I took the medicine, it tasted sour and cool. 'It's odd to find a hyperplasia in such a young girl!' the pharmacist commented in surprise.

'Yes, it is, isn't it?' said Mum.

Her colleague asked: 'How did you discover it?'

'She found it herself when she was scratching.'

We used to play at sex back then. Of course it was just a game. The books say so: when boys and girls play at having sex it's just a game and grown-ups shouldn't worry because children are not physically mature enough for real sex. Lili and I started to play same-sex games when I was six and she was seven. Lili was our neighbour, and her mother was from Beijing. It was all because of the models and charts up in the attic, and because of babies being born. My mother did family planning education, and the flesh-coloured models – male and female sex organs made of plastic or plaster of Paris – were stored up there, a jumble of peculiar, mysterious objects. When I was bored in the afternoons, I used to sneak upstairs and look at them. The models were cross-sectioned and some had sinister, blood-coloured insides, but most were flesh-pink, some soft when you prodded them, others hard. If I heard a noise, I'd break out in a sweat. But as soon as it was quiet again, I screwed up my courage and took a good look. I was all alone. The adults had been despatched to the countryside and when I started my explorations, Lili hadn't moved in. I was one little girl standing amid a jumbled heap of sex education models. It must have been quite a strange sight. Did anyone in the whole world ever have a childhood like this?

When I think back, I see the models as flowers blooming on the dark floor of the attic, and I see myself, hunkered down in front of them, staring intently.

I was very excited by the idea of seeing a baby being born. The hospital delivery room windows were covered by dark blue curtains and the windows were placed high up, so you had to climb up to get a look inside. I couldn't climb and standing on tiptoe wasn't any good. I could step back a bit and jump in the air and crane my neck but still I couldn't see anything. I really needed a gust of wind to blow the curtains aside just when I was in midair, but I never got lucky. There was another window which directly faced the delivery table, but you had to go round the back of the building, and squeeze through the thornbushes that guarded the walls. The ground was littered with broken glass, and you might be spotted by the grown-ups too. It was awfully risky and complicated, and then you had to get to the window at the precise moment when a woman was giving birth. Finally, just one time, everything came together and I got to the window and the curtains hadn't been drawn and a woman was lying on the delivery table with her legs wide open, just as if the sex education models in the attic had come to life on a woman's body. Her legs were wide as they could be, everything was in full view. The sight terrified me. She looked like some weird painting that you were used to seeing hanging motionless on the wall until suddenly one day a figure in it sat up and walked out of the picture. I was so scared that my arms and legs went limp and I tumbled to the ground. By the time I climbed back up again, the curtains were drawn and I couldn't see anything. I heard voices inside, the clatter of metal instruments, and running water.

How did babies come out? It was a mystery. Once I heard about a woman who'd had a baby outdoors. She was in labour and just as she was hobbling across a sports ground, the baby tumbled out. Lots of people saw it, in fact there were so many rubberneckers crowded onto the stone terraces, they could hardly see past each other. After the woman and her baby were taken away, people dispersed and you could see a gleaming puddle of dark red blood on one of the benches. It was a dangerous business having a baby. Women bled and sometimes they died. That was something I learnt early on. And dangerous things had always fascinated me. I was forever waiting, in a mixture of trepidation and excitement, for dangerous times to come, as if they were something to celebrate.

I must have secretly been a masochist.

All those years when I was a child, I never did see a birth. Childbirth happened near where we lived, in the obstetrics and gynaecology department, with its sparse shade of loquat trees. My mum used to say you got a run of boys one day and all girls the next, popping out like strings of beads. It was all predetermined, they came out like an ikebana flower arrangement. Then the calm would be shattered as a baby with no head or two heads was born. The deformed foetuses would be wrapped in bright yellow coarse paper and collected by odd-job men in white overalls, who buried them in shallow graves on the hillside behind the hospital. Sometimes wild dogs dug them up during the night. When grown-ups died, they were buried there too. It had to be that particular hill because the mountains further off were all stone. These were the strange beautiful rock formations typical of Guilin; it was magical scenery but you couldn't bury anyone there, there was no earth. Snail Ridge, that was the name of the burial ground, and it was a mysterious, frightening place. Later on, air-raid shelters were dug on Snail Ridge. The diggers turned up large numbers of white human skulls, so old that no one knew who they were. We children were taken to look during the day. The trenches were waist-deep on a grown-up, and over the head of a child, and at the bottom, the air was close and the earth smelled cold and clammy. When the shelters were completed, we had night-time air-raid drills in B Township: when the sirens sounded, we were all, old and young alike, hauled out of bed and told to dress in dark clothes. Then we were marched swiftly up the hill and into the shelters. No torches or matches were allowed, or crying or shouting. It was a practice drill every time, but it always felt real.

The hospital entrance was on a main road, and that was the

way the bodies were taken out when they were going to be buried, there was no other way. Sometimes the dead person would be accompanied by half-a-dozen family members, wearing white cloth shoes and white headbands, weeping and wailing. That was when it was an old person from B Township. Sometimes, there were ranks of officials with black armbands, carrying funeral wreaths, when a government official had died. They passed our door on their way to the morgue. Then the morgue door opened and a black or dark-red coffin emerged, and they all set off up the hillside. The slopes were covered in a kind of tree with small creamy-coloured flowers and long, thin leaves that had a bad smell. I don't know what they were called. Funeral wreaths in B Township were always woven from the twigs and leaves of that tree.

Our toilets in the hospital compound were almost next door to the morgue, with only a weed-filled, overgrown courtyard in between. When I went to the toilet, I used to think of the morgue right behind me, and on gloomy days and dark nights, I thought of the ghosts flitting around on the other side of the wall. What did ghosts look like? I wondered.

At one time, I was always imagining dying. My grandmother used to say: 'If only your dad wasn't dead, you'd have as many sweeties and biscuits as you wanted.'

'What's dead?' I asked.

'Your dad's dead, that means you won't see him anymore.'

'Why did he die?'

'He got ill,' she told me.

'If he hadn't got ill, he wouldn't be dead?'

'We all die sometime.'

'When am I going to die?' I asked.

'Not for years and years. You're just a little girl, Duomi. You haven't grown up yet.'

'When will you die, Gran?'

'Soon. I'm old.'

'I get it,' I said. 'You'll die and then Mum and then me... Are you afraid of dying?'

'No, I'm not afraid, I'm old,' she told me.

My nights were filled with dreams. I used to dream that someone in my family died, sometimes my gran, but usually my mum. She'd be like a famous woman revolutionary in the movies, I'd hear the clattering of chains, or she'd be hit by a stray bullet and fall to the ground, or I'd see her mangled corpse pouring blood. I was quite clear, in my dream, that if my mother died, I'd be a proper orphan and I was only eight years old, so how would I look after myself? I'd wake up in a cold sweat, even though I knew it as just a dream and by waking up I'd escaped from that horrible place. I knew my mother wasn't really dead, she'd just been sent to work in the countryside. I wasn't an orphan but my gran had gone back to the village too, and I spent the nights alone at home. On those nights, I was still terrified, even though my mum and gran were still alive. There was nothing but my quilt to stop me having nightmares as soon as I shut my eyes.

Later on, I dreamt it was me dying.

I was always being chased, and no matter how I tried to run and hide, I was always caught and escorted to a very high wall, where I stood with gun muzzles pointing at me. At the instant they took aim, I'd think to myself: *This is it, I'm going to die. I'll never come back to life again.* A red flash and my chest burned, and in my dream, I really would die.

Apart from dreams of dying, my other worst nightmares were of getting married. I have no idea why a little kid would dream about that. In my imagination, marriage was something terrifying. I was sure I'd never get married, I wasn't that kind of person, but in my dreams, I was being trapped by some gigantic force and married against my will. My dreams were always of the wedding, married life never featured; kids always think of marriage as a wedding. It was just as I'd seen adults getting married in real life: I would be made to stand at a big table, and someone would be telling me: 'This is your marriage.' The bridegroom standing beside me would be the nastiest boy in my class or else the ugliest man in B Township and I'd wake up with a start, covered in sweat. Still half-asleep and confused, I'd think to myself: *Oh no, this is it!* I suppose really I was afraid of the nasty boy or ugly man.

There was another dream that came back again and again, invariably when I got sick and had a temperature, right up until I was eight years old. It was an abstract dream, there was no story to it, and to this day I have no idea what it was about. But it recurred so many times that I remember it clearly, the images and colours as bright as the colours of the spectrum: red, orange, yellow, green, turquoise, blue and purple. The colour shapes varied, sometimes like a rainbow, long, thin stripes, only straight, not curved; or short and stubby; or vertical, reaching right into my dreams from some far distant place, flooding the space. Sometimes the colours came fast and were dense, tightly packed together, which I didn't like at all; then they arrived in a slow trickle, and then they were more vivid, a long stretch of red, and then of yellow, sliding gently in. I found that more pleasant. Sometimes, the colours arrived with such a rush that my head felt like it was splitting, and even when they slowed down, I felt like I was drowning until I bobbed up to the surface of the water. Sometimes I had this dream when I just felt unwell but didn't have a temperature. I was a sickly child, always coming down with something or another, so I often had this dream.

Where did the colours of rainbows come from?

When the rainbow dream came, I was always on my own. My mother was never there, as she was only home for a few days a year. When I was sick, I had to look after myself. I drank water, went to sleep and had my rainbow dream. I didn't take any medicine. Even then, I knew that taking medicines built up drug resistance, so that when you were really sick they wouldn't work anymore. I had no neighbours, they all slept in the Epidemic Prevention Station. My mother had been transferred to a new job in Women and Children's Health Care, where there were just four workers, including the director. With all the adults working on the communes, I was left in our house, a long narrow building of four floors. The ground floor was occupied by another family's housekeeper, and I slept alone on level three. It was an oddly shaped house, with two long, narrow rooms on each floor. No doubt it had once been an inn. Next door was a salt warehouse, and the base of the walls were covered in chunks of saltpetre. So there I was, three floors up, in a dark, deserted house, with all the colours of the rainbow coming out of another darkness and endlessly invading my dreams.

That particular dream vanished after I was eight years old, and never returned even when I had a temperature. More than twenty years later, the year I turned thirty, my then-boyfriend gave me a black clock as a present. It was small and square, and fitted neatly in the palm of my hand. One night I realised that rays of light were coming off the clock face and being reflected in faint rainbow hues on the shiny tabletop. There were rainbow colours both on the clock face and the tabletop, it was a very strange sight. I was suddenly reminded of my childhood dream. I still don't know why these two objects were linked so mysteriously. After I broke up with my boyfriend, it suddenly struck me that there was something very sinister about the clock: the long white clock hands on the black background were like the white whiskers of a black cat, and seemed as treacherous as time itself.

Over and over again, I died in my dreams, and came back to life when I woke up again. In summer, my nights began at half past five. The Epidemic Prevention Station cafeteria served dinner at four-thirty and there was nothing much to do after that, unless I went to the park to pick azuki beans. Then I'd be in bed a little after eight. Or half past five, if I didn't go anywhere after eating. No one was looking after me and I had nowhere to go. I was scared, alone in the house. Only my bed felt secure. When I pulled down the mosquito nets, it was not to go to sleep but to give me a space where I was safe. What really terrified me was to go to bed after darkness had fallen. Coming in from outside, I had to go along a dark corridor. The only area that was lit was the courtyard at the back of the building, but I wasn't going that far. I climbed the stairs from the first courtyard, my footsteps echoing in the darkness. I was sure there was someone behind me, and I would look around every second step. There was a light when the stairs turned the corner but the bulb had burnt out long ago. Around the bend, if I looked up, I could see the sky framed by the courtyard walls, a faint patch of stars. As I neared the top, my footsteps no longer sounded so loud but I was still anxious as I climbed. Three floors up, I opened my door, turned the light on and inspected behind the door and under the bed. Then I pushed two bolts across the door – and I could relax. The toilet was right at the end of the building, in the third courtyard, so I never had a drink in the evening, so I wouldn't need to go to the toilet.

If I went to bed at half past five, I didn't feel so afraid. At that time of day, the sun hadn't set and its rays still shone on the wall behind the bed. There was light all around me when I pulled the mosquito net down, and that made me feel completely secure. I could banish the darkness outside the room, I'd be safe inside by the time night fell. Sometimes I would sit up in bed, motionless, my back icy cold, or I would lie down as the light turned from gold to pale, then grey. The dusk was very peaceful. Then came darkness. I heaved a sigh of relief. Sometimes, I even went to sleep when it was still light and would wake up in the middle of the night, thinking about death, thinking I was falling down a long, dark tunnel, from which I would never get out again.

New Titles from Giramondo

Fiction

Pip Adam *Audition*
Sanya Rushdi *Hospital*
Alexis Wright *Praiseworthy*
Shaun Prescott *The Town*
Jon Fosse *Septology* (trans. Damion Searls)
Shaun Prescott *Bon and Lesley*
George Alexander *Mortal Divide: The Autobiography of Yiorgos Alexandroglou*
Luke Carman *An Ordinary Ecstasy*
Norman Erikson Pasaribu *Happy Stories, Mostly* (trans. Tiffany Tsao)
Jessica Au *Cold Enough for Snow*

Non-fiction

Imants Tillers *Credo*
Bastian Fox Phelan *How to Be Between*
Antigone Kefala *Late Journals*
Evelyn Juers *The Dancer: A Biography for Philippa Cullen*
Gerald Murnane *Last Letter to a Reader*

Poetry

Louise Carter *Golden Repair*
π.O. *The Tour*
Luke Beesley *In the Photograph*
Grace Yee *Chinese Fish*
Autumn Royal *The Drama Student*
Lucy Dougan *Monster Field*
Michael Farrell *Googlecholia*
Lisa Gorton *Mirabilia*
Zheng Xiaoqiong *In the Roar of the Machine* (trans. Eleanor Goodman)
Lionel Fogarty *Harvest Lingo*
Tracy Ryan *Rose Interior*
Claire Potter *Acanthus*
Adam Aitken *Revenants*

For more information visit giramondopublishing.com.

Acknowledgements

We respectfully acknowledge the Gadigal, Burramattagal and Cammeraygal peoples, the traditional owners of the lands where Giramondo's offices are located. We extend our respects to their ancestors and to all First Nations peoples and Elders.

HEAT Series 3 Number 10 has been prepared in collaboration with Ligare Book Printers and Candida Stationery; we thank them for their support.

The Giramondo Publishing Company is grateful for the support of Western Sydney University in the implementation of its book publishing program.

Giramondo Publishing is assisted by the Australian Government through the Australia Council for the Arts.

This project is supported by the Copyright Agency's Cultural Fund.

HEAT Series 3
Editor Alexandra Christie
Designer Jenny Grigg
Typesetter Andrew Davies
Copyeditor Aleesha Paz
Marketing Manager Kate Prendergast
Publishers Ivor Indyk and Evelyn Juers
Associate Publisher Nick Tapper

Editorial Advisory Board
Chris Andrews, Mieke Chew, J.M. Coetzee, Lucy Dougan, Lisa Gorton,
Bella Li, Tamara Sampey-Jawad, Suneeta Peres da Costa, Alexis Wright
and Ashleigh Young.

Contact
For editorial enquiries, please email
heat.editor@giramondopublishing.com.
Follow us on Instagram @HEAT.lit and
Twitter @HEAT_journal.

Accessibility
We understand that some formats will not be accessible to all readers.
If you are a reader with specific access requirements, please contact
orders@giramondopublishing.com.

For more information, visit giramondopublishing.com/heat.

Published August 2023
from the Writing and Society Research Centre
at Western Sydney University
by the Giramondo Publishing Company
Locked Bag 1797
Penrith NSW 2751 Australia
www.giramondopublishing.com

This collection © Giramondo Publishing 2023
Typeset in Tiempos and Founders Grotesk Condensed
designed by Kris Sowersby at Klim Type Foundry

Printed and bound by Ligare Book Printers
Distributed in Australia by NewSouth Books

A catalogue record for this book is available from
the National Library of Australia.

HEAT Series 3 Number 10
ISBN: 978-1-922725-09-7
ISSN: 1326-1460